The Tree of
Ecstasy
and
Unbearable
Sadness

Dirt Lane Press Inc.
PO Box 876, Orange NSW Australia 2800.

www.dirtlanepress.com

Published by Dirt Lane Press Inc 2021.
Text and illustrations copyright © Matt Ottley 2021.
Music © Matt Ottley 2020.
First published 2021.

 A catalogue record for this
book is available from the
National Library of Australia

ISBN: 978-0-6480238-5-2

Cover and internal design by Hannah Janzen.
Typesetting by Hannah Janzen.
Additional design by Tina Wilson.

Original artwork photographed by Mark Lutz, Art House Reproductions.

The quote from Charlotte Guest's poem 'Notes on the Disappearance
of a Friend,' is published in *Soap*, Recent Work Press, Canberra, 2017.

Produced and printed through Asia Pacific Offset.

Printed in China

5 4 3 2 1

There is a CD in the back of the book containing a 50-minute
work for orchestra and choir with full narration of the text.
This musical work is also available as a free digital
download at www.mattottley.com/downloads

The Tree of *Ecstasy* and *Unbearable Sadness*

MATT
OTTLEY

DIRT
LANE
PRESS

In loving memory of
Gabriella Silipo

In time, it becomes bearable:
this is the most unbearable part.

From the poem Notes on
the Disappearance of a Friend
by Charlotte Guest

PART ONE
Genesis

Even before he was born, he was cherished.

But there was, even then, deep within him, a seed.

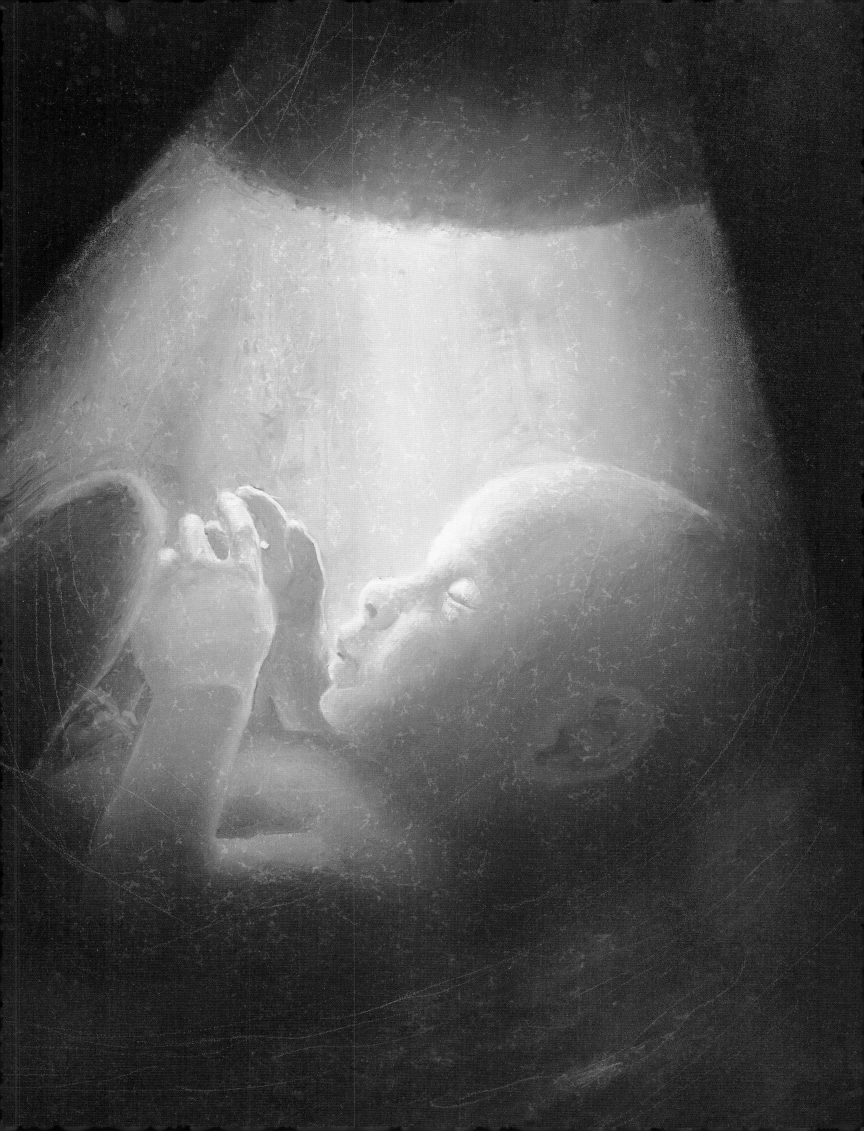

As the seed sprouted ...

and grew ...

it made the boy see things invisible to others.

Some people called him odd,
others eccentric.

Children teased him.
His friendships didn't last long.

'What's wrong with me?'
he asked his parents.

'Nothing, darling,' his mother said,
'you see and feel things differently
to others.'

'Perhaps this is a gift,' suggested
his father.

His gift showed him things so beautiful
they made him cry.

But it also tormented him with the pain
of others that made him feel numb.

When his sadness became unbearable,
his parents sought the help of doctors.

They proclaimed there was a tree, whose flower was ecstasy, and whose fruit was sadness, growing within him.

It would always be there.

But they could give him medicine to
stop the tree flowering and fruiting ...
and for a time the medicine worked.

The tree, however, continued to grow ...

and eventually became more powerful
than the medicine.

One day, the effort of containing
the tree became too difficult.

'Please,' implored his friends,
'you must fight.'

'You mustn't allow yourself to
be lost,' cried his parents.

'The tree is too strong for me,'
said the boy.

Soon he could not even speak.

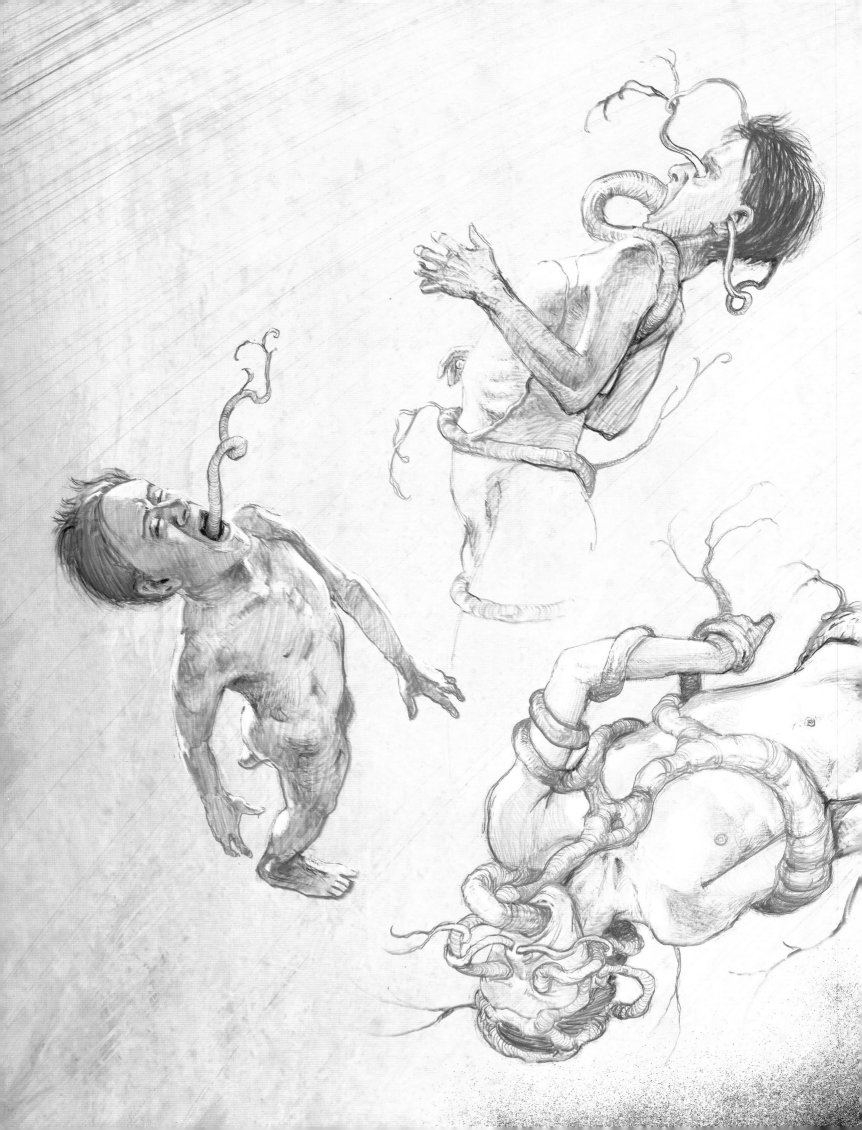

And not long after that there
was nothing of him but the tree.

PART TWO
Metamorphosis

His mind, however, was now ...

released.

Under the vast dome of the sky and across thundering oceans he flew.

He saw many things:
beasts of the ether that
raged around him.

But he pushed against the storm and soon found himself in a drifting place of light and emptiness.

Eventually he emerged
into a world of beauty
and wonder.

PART THREE
Ascension

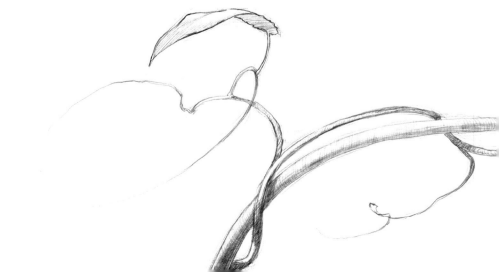

He journeyed until he came upon an ancient city.

At the heart of the city was a palace,
where, within its tremendous stone walls,
he met a powerful sovereign.

He perched on her shoulder.

'Hello,' he sang.

'Insolence,' the sovereign cried. 'You must bow before me.
Not sing! I shall have your wings clipped!'

'I ... I didn't know,' the boy stammered. 'I'm not from here.'

'What do you mean?' demanded the sovereign. 'You are
not making sense! There is nowhere but here! This is *It*.
The Place. *Here.*' She glared at him for a moment.
'Now. Start again. You must pray.'

'But to whom?'

The sovereign quivered with indignation. 'To *me*, of course! *I* am The One Who Governs. *I* am The Bubble and *I* am the Holy Cake of Soap! Only through *me* are the people cleansed. Now ... *adorate* me.'

The boy bowed and clasped his wings.
'I ... pray to thee,' he began,
'The One Who Governs, The Bubble
and the Holy Cake of Soap.'

'You are still guilty!' the sovereign interrupted.
'What shall We do with you?'

The boy squirmed.

'*Well?*' she shouted.

He chirped nervously.
But could think of nothing.

'I know!' the sovereign declared.
'You shall be banished to travel the far reaches
of my realm, in search of ... of ... of ...'

'Of beauty?' suggested the boy.

'Yes, beauty!' said the sovereign,
pleased with herself. 'And you must
report back everything you see that
divinely reflects me. That is *The Rule.*'

The boy flew out of the city into the valleys and amongst the hills of Here, to begin his atonement.

PART FOUR
Fragility

He saw many strange
and beautiful things.

He came upon a flower whose allure was
so powerful he longed, beyond anything,
to be devoured by it.

But he was not ready for such beauty.

On a high mountain pass, one whose face was winsome with the passage of her long years, told him that two nights thence, when the moon was full, the Tree of Perspicacious Lanterns would sing – a once-in-one-thousand-year occurrence.

And so it did.

The tree's flowers glowed like lanterns
and a melody, ethereal and mysterious,
shimmered up its trunk to resound from
the flowers in a thousand voices.

The boy ached to grasp hold of the
sound, and wept at its utter beauty.

He stumbled to the tree ... but at his touch the voices ceased and the light in every lantern went out.

A cry echoed from deep in the tree's roots. Its branches began to curl and wilt.

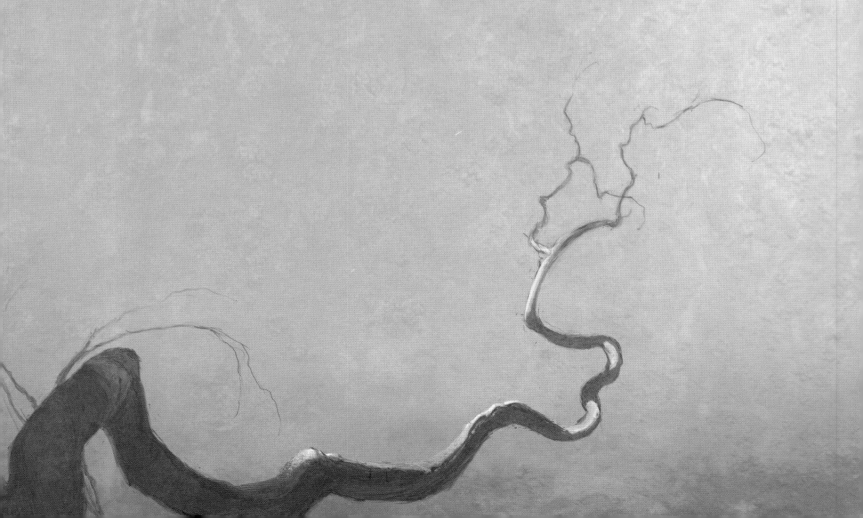

The boy ran from the valley.

'I have destroyed life,' he wailed,
appalled by the force of his desire and
by the destructive power of his touch.

In the days that followed he saw delicacy in everything.

But his dismay at the fragility of things was gradually tempered by their beauty. Sad as he was, he felt his being blossom with warmth and love.

PART FIVE
Revelation

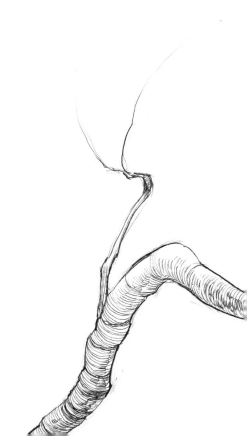

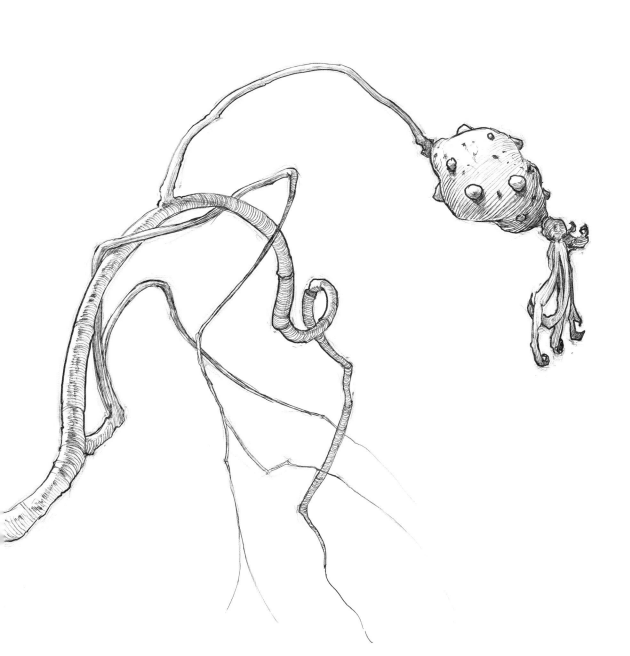

He wandered through the seasons and came to
a place where water thundered into mist. He could
not see what lay beyond.

'Maybe this is the edge of the world,' he thought.

Then he saw something unexpected.
In all his wandering of the wilderness,
he hadn't seen another human, but there ...
ahead of him ... were people.

And what the boy discovered
beyond the mist and roaring water
made him turn back at once.

'I must warn The One Who
Governs!' he said to himself.

He flew back through the valleys
and over the hills of Here until
he reached the city.

'I have seen and heard many strange and beautiful things,' he told the sovereign. 'I now know the dimensions of your domain, and I have seen the fragility of all things.' He paused to gather his courage. 'But I have discovered something else. You are *not* The Ruler of *All* Things.'

'What do you mean?' the sovereign demanded.

'I've found the edge of the world,' the boy persevered, 'but it isn't actually the edge. There is a land beyond the edge, and you and your people are not alone. You have neighbours.'

'And?' she spluttered.

'Unlike your people,' the boy said, 'who wear wigs in public, your neighbours wear pompoms. Also, your neighbours pray to a giant roasted chicken that sits in a volcano. No one has actually ever seen this chicken, but they are sure it's there. It roasted itself to ensure the perpetual good nourishment of the people.'

'It makes no sense!' the sovereign cried. '*I* am The Ruler of *All* Things! You are lying! I shall have you plucked.'

'You ... you must believe me,' cried the boy bravely. 'Not only that, your neighbours are numerous in number, so numerous they have crept into your realm.'

'*Outrageous!*' the sovereign bellowed. 'And as for their pompoms, they are breaking The Rules,' breaking The Rules.'

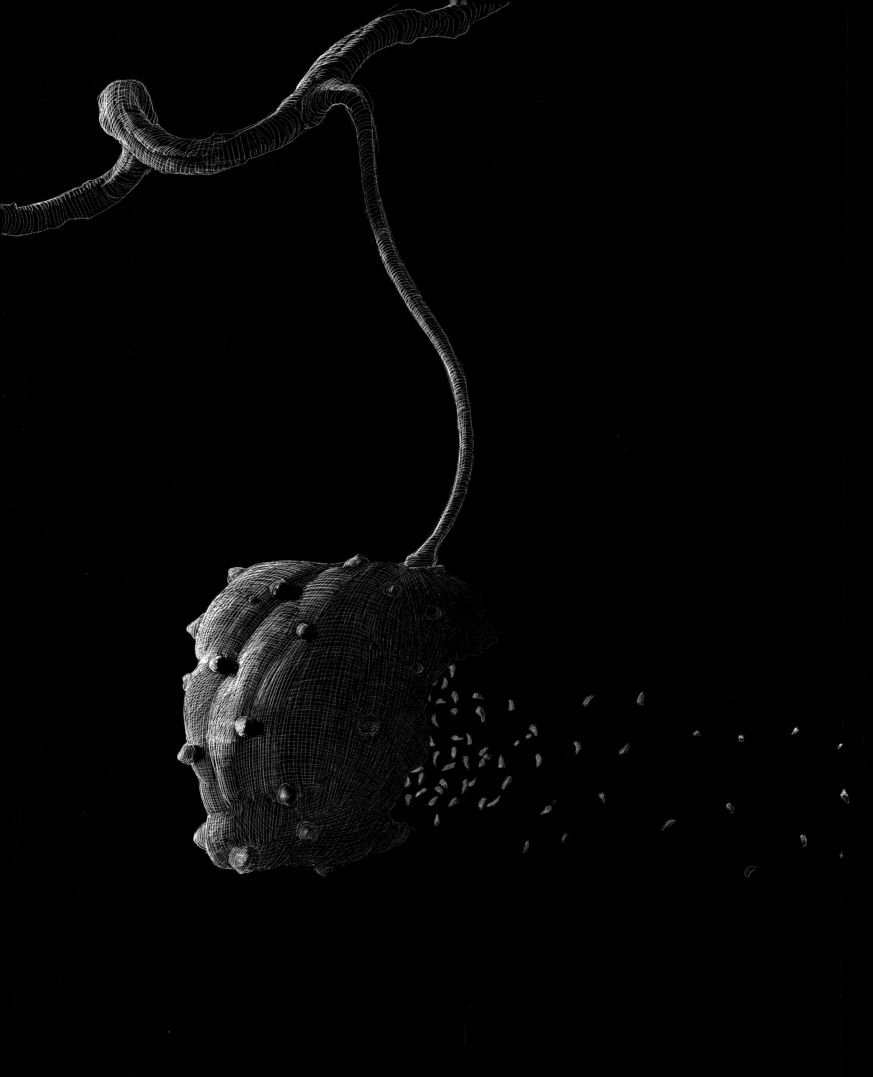

PART SIX
Tempest

A terrible conflict began.

At first the combatants attacked each
other with nothing but their own bodies.

Then as the war spread and intensified,
they made machines of destruction that
tore open the land and released storms
and diseases to rage across the world.

The boy was appalled by what he'd unleashed.
His anger and despair rose until it clawed the
clouds and tried to tear down the sky itself
to smother and obliterate all he'd done.

His screams of fury and anguish
stilled even the storms.

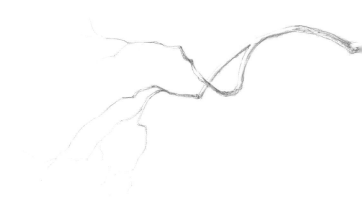

PART SEVEN
Quietude

In the silence that followed he heard distant voices, the voices of those who loved him.

He was once again within his tree, where, with all the grief of his heart, he pushed against his entombment.

'I am here,' he called.

And so he came back into the world.

And still the Tree of Ecstasy and
Unbearable Sadness was within him.

And still it grew flowers.

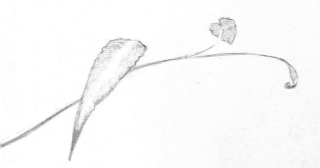

And still it bore fruit.

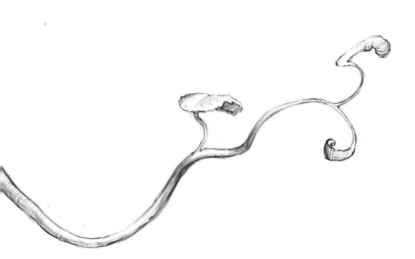

MUSIC CREDITS

Composition/Orchestration – Matt Ottley

Guest composition – Alf Demasi

Project Manager/Narrator – Tina Wilson
Solo Tenor – Benjamin Reynolds
Production – First Creative Ltd
Producer/Engineer – Jaroslav Zouhar
Mixing/Mastering – Dave Rowell
Score preparation – Clifford Bradley, Jigsaw Music

ORCHESTRA

Brno Philharmonic Orchestra
Conductor – Mikel Toms
Concertmaster – Pavel Wallinger
www.filharmonie-brno.cz/en/

CHOIR

Czech Philharmonic Choir of Brno
Choir director – Petr Fiala
Chorusmaster – Jan Svejkovský
ARS/KONCERT director – Hana Svobodová
Artist Manager – Marie Keprtová

www.cfsbrno.cz/
www.arskoncert.cz/

Orchestra and Choir recorded at the Besední dům,
Brno, Czech Republic

Recording of narration – Marc Mittag, Kingdom of Kunghur Studios

Score published by One Tentacle Publishing

LYRICS

PART 4 – FRAGILITY

Tenor:
Light eternal
I have yearned for thee
For one thousand years
I have railed in fear
Shine on those
I have thrown stones upon
Sisters
Brothers
Blood of my heart
Shine upon the dark
Let me find in thee
Light eternal
Light eternal
I have yearned for thee

Choir:
Lux aeterna (light eternal)

PART 6 – TEMPEST

Tenor:
I am
Anger
Hatred
I am
Loathing
Rage
Annihilation
I am
The day of reckoning
Ah ... Ah ... Ah ... Ah
I am
Annihilation
I am
Anger
I am
Hatred
Loathing
Fear

Choir:
Dies irae (Day of wrath)
Dies illa (That day)

PART 7 – QUIETUDE

Tenor:
Hear me
Feel my presence
I am here
Hear me
I am here
I am here
© Matt Ottley

Choir:
Hear me
Feel me

ACKNOWLEDGEMENTS

My deepest gratitude to the following
people for their support in this project:
Sam Silipo, Tina Wilson, Margrete Lamond,
Jennie Orchard, Alf Demasi and Margaret
Kennedy.

I would also like to thank all the
staff between 2010 and 2014 of the
Alma Street Clinic, Fremantle, WA.

My heartfelt thanks to Rae Kennedy,
Kath Arno, Lesley & Bob Reece, Danny
& Judy Parker, Mailee Clarke and Heather
McClelland.

THE PHILANTHROPIC TRUST

The Gabby Arts Legacy Trust (GALT) is a philanthropic trust set up in memory of Gabriella Silipo (or Gabby, as she was known by her friends). The Trust aims to make a significant contribution to the arts and society in Australia, primarily by funding worthy and innovative arts projects that it deems as having cultural and social value. The ultimate aspirational outcome is for the creative endeavour to be a catalyst for beneficial change for all humankind, be that benefit great or small.

GALT is honoured to support both the musical and production components of *The Tree of Ecstasy and Unbearable Sadness*. GALT's hope and anticipation is that this exciting project will both spark and encourage ongoing discussion around its various challenging themes, and will offer reassurance to young people struggling with the social isolation so often associated with mental illness.

To experience this work as intended
by the author, you are invited
to listen to the accompanying music
while re-reading the book.

Or, now you have read the book, listen
to the music with your eyes closed.

The CD contains a 50-minute work
for orchestra, choir and solo tenor
with full narration of the text.
The music is an auditory exploration
of the themes in the book.

A digital download is available for free from:
www.mattottley.com/downloads